Ancient Maya

Archaeology Unlocks the Secrets of the Maya's Past

Ancient Maya

Archaeology Unlocks the Secrets of the Maya's Past

By Nathaniel Harris

Elizabeth Graham, Consultant

NATIONAL
GEOGRAPHIC
Washington, DC

Contents

1

2

3

4

< In this Maya carving made in Yaxchilan in about 725, a queen, bottom right, has made
a sacrifice to summon a Vision Serpent with a warrior emerging from its jaws.

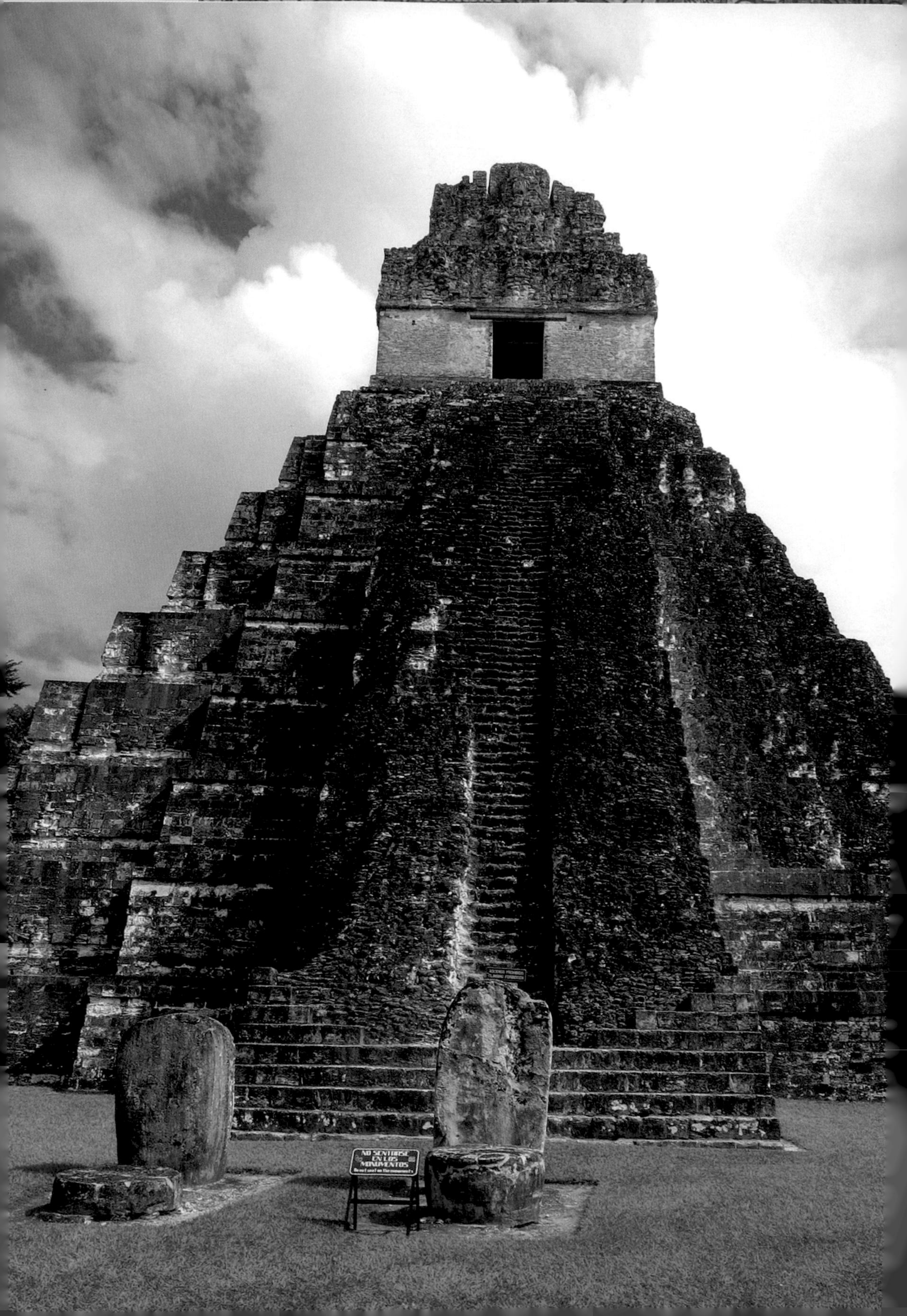
NO SENTARSE
EN LOS
MONUMENTOS

< Temple I at Tikal has nine levels rising to the shrine on top: Nine was a sacred number for the Maya. Tikal's five great temples were originally painted white.

From the Consultant

The land of the Maya encompasses the places we now know as Chiapas and the Yucatán in Mexico, Guatemala, Belize, and the western parts of Honduras and El Salvador. The Maya were not a single group. Before the coming of the Europeans, people did not use the general term "Maya." Instead, the individuals and groups who lived in the region identified themselves in similar ways to the ways we use today: By family name or place of residence, by regional or kinship ties, or in terms of language and culture. Today as in the past, however, the Maya also have things in common despite these differences. Mayan languages are all related to different degrees, and cultural factors also tie Mayan-speaking peoples together. At the same time, those factors distinguish Mayan speakers from other peoples of the region, such as the Mexica (Aztec), Zapotec, Pipil, or Otomí.

These distinctive cultural factors form much of the subject matter of this book: Mayan writing and its use by kings and queens to glorify their dynasties and their rule; the Maya calendar and the astronomers who kept track so accurately of the movements of the heavenly bodies; Maya architecture and the distinctive urban environment of Maya cities; Maya rulers and their elaborate burials; Maya views of the dead and the afterlife; widespread networks of trade and exchange; and Maya agriculture and culinary practices.

Many of these cultural factors still survive. As you will see in this book, although the Spanish conquest changed much of Precolumbian life, the Maya still occupy and are rooted in the lands of their ancestors.

Elizabeth Graham,
London, 2007

Elizabeth Graham makes notes at a Maya site at Lamanai in Belize, where she has directed excavations since 1997. The site may yield a sequence of dates that will help clarify the chronology of the later period of Maya history, known as the Postclassic.

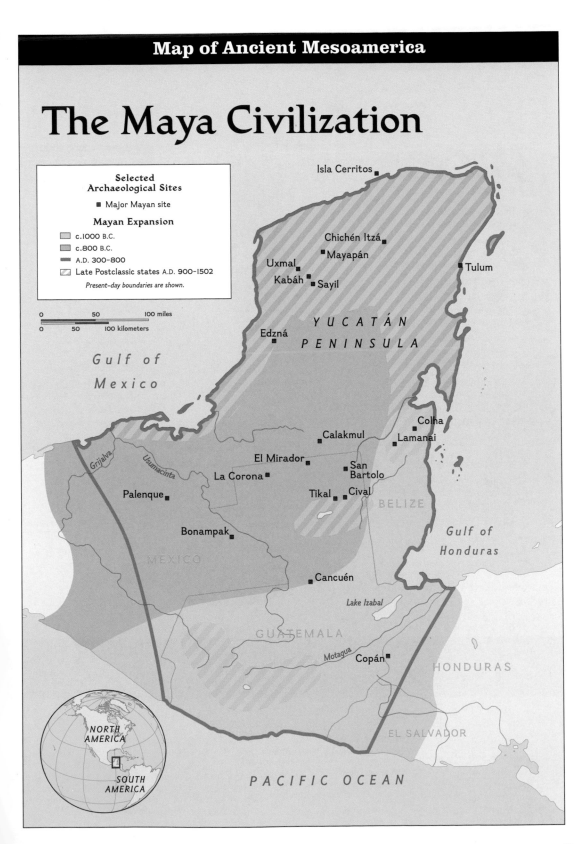

Map of Ancient Mesoamerica

The Maya Civilization

Selected Archaeological Sites

■ Major Mayan site

Mayan Expansion

- c.1000 B.C.
- c.800 B.C.
- A.D. 300–800
- Late Postclassic states A.D. 900–1502

Present-day boundaries are shown.

0   50   100 miles
0   50   100 kilometers

Gulf of Mexico

Isla Cerritos

Chichén Itzá
Mayapán
Uxmal
Kabáh Sayil
Tulum

Edzná

YUCATÁN
PENINSULA

Grijalva

Usumacinta

Calakmul
Colha
Lamanai

El Mirador
San Bartolo
La Corona
Tikal   Cival
Palenque
BELIZE

Bonampak

MEXICO

Gulf of Honduras

Cancuén

Lake Izabal

GUATEMALA

Motagua   Copán
HONDURAS

NORTH AMERICA

SOUTH AMERICA

EL SALVADOR

PACIFIC OCEAN

9

THREE MAJOR PERIODS OF
Maya History

Preclassic

ca 1500 B.C—A.D. 250

The Maya emerged from villages in the lowlands of Mesoamerica and later the Yucatán. By 1000 B.C. they were burying their dead with pieces of pottery and jewelry. The early Maya came under the influence of the Olmec from the Gulf Coast of Mexico, who may have influenced Maya ideas about kingship. By the late Preclassic, Maya kings were being buried in elaborate tombs full of valuable artifacts. The Maya developed writing in symbols called glyphs by 300 B.C. By the end of the Preclassic, large lowland cities such as El Mirador and Tikal had been built.

> This pottery vessel was found in the oldest-known Maya royal tomb, which dates from about 150 B.C.

Classic

ca A.D. 250—900

The Classic is sometimes divided into Early Classic and Late Classic at about A.D. 600. Maya society became more specialized, with farmers, craftsmen, and traders, and powerful dynasties who dominated cities such as Tikal, Copán, and Palenque. Trade among the cities was common: But so was warfare. Some Maya may have come under the influence of Teotihuacan in central Mexico. Early in the 9th century, however, political collapse seems to have struck the main cities of the lowlands. By the end of the century they had been abandoned.

Timeline of Mesoamerican History

1500 B.C.

1000

500

B.C. 0 A.D.

ca 1500 B.C.
Villages emerge in southern Mexico, marking the start of the Preclassical period

ca 1200 B.C.
The Olmec build San Lorenzo on the Gulf of Mexico

ca 1000 B.C.
Maya peoples move into the Yucatán

ca 600 B.C.
Maya centers emerge at Cobá and Copán

CA 500 B.C.
The Maya drink chocolate made from cacao

ca 350 B.C.
City-states emerge

300 B.C.
The Maya develop writing

100 B.C.
Murals are painted at San Bartolo in Guatemala

A.

Preclassic Period

< This elaborate stone lance head was carved in the middle of the eighth century. It was probably part of a lance carried by the king as a sign of his authority.

Postclassic

ca A.D. 900–1500

The focus of Maya culture moved north to the Yucatán, where Classic styles continued in upland cities such as Uxmal and Kabah. Chichén (or Chichén Itzá) was a dominant power in the centuries just before or after 1000, and reflected the influence of the Toltec from central Mexico. Chichén's dominance then passed to Mayapán before it was destroyed in 1441. Maya civilization survived, even after the arrival of the Spaniards in the Yucatán in 1528, but without the political unity or power to rival the achievements of the past.

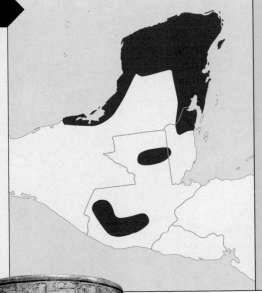

< This vase from the Classic period is decorated with glyphs and images of warriors in battle.

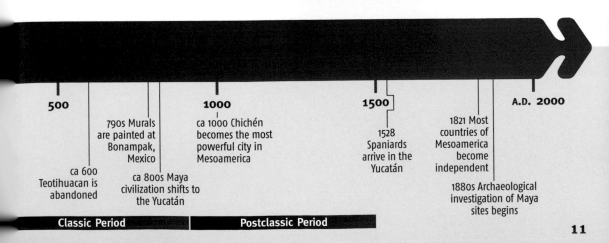

500		1000		1500		A.D. 2000

790s Murals are painted at Bonampak, Mexico

ca 1000 Chichén becomes the most powerful city in Mesoamerica

1528 Spaniards arrive in the Yucatán

1821 Most countries of Mesoamerica become independent

ca 600 Teotihuacan is abandoned

ca 800s Maya civilization shifts to the Yucatán

1880s Archaeological investigation of Maya sites begins

Classic Period   **Postclassic Period**

Yesterday Comes Alive

CHAPTER 1

How do we learn what we know about the past?

Marcello Canuto wanted to escape. Mosquitos were everywhere—and they were hungry. The Yale University scholar was waiting for his global positioning device to tell him exactly where he was in the rain forest of northern Guatemala. The device uses signals from satellites in space orbit to pinpoint locations on the Earth's surface. Canuto was part of a team exploring a group of ancient ruins named La Corona in 2005. An earlier expedition had identified La Corona as the likely location of one of the great mysteries of Guatemala's history: Site Q.

< Workers remove the carved Maya panel discovered by Marcello Canuto deep in a trench at the site at La Corona.

∧ Marcello Canuto examines the carved piece of limestone he found at La Corona.

< The glyphs on the panel from La Corona shared similar characteristics with carvings from the mysterious location known only as Site Q. Experts had to compare the style with other panels to work out that they all came from the same place.

A lasting mystery

Scholars knew Site Q existed only from stone panels that began to turn up in museums around the world in the 1960s. The panels were carved with script and drawings created by the Maya who lived in what are now Guatemala, Belize, and parts of Mexico from 1500 B.C. to the 15th century, and whose descendants still live there.

Thousands of Maya carvings were known, but the new panels were remarkable. They looked as fresh as the day they were made. Expert Peter Matthews identified 30 artifacts in different collections that he believed came from the same source. But no one knew where that source was. The pieces had been removed from the site by looters and sold on the black market. Matthews named the mystery source Site Q, short for the Spanish word "que?", or "which?"

Looters help out

Marcello Canuto was on the last day of his expedition to La Corona when the mosquitos struck. He took refuge in a trench left by looters digging for ancient artifacts to sell. The looters had given up, but Canuto realized that they had given up too easily. Soil had fallen away at the end of the trench to reveal a small chamber. In the gloom, Canuto could see a white limestone panel about 3 feet by 1.5 feet (90 by 50 cm) carved with about 40 oblong symbols. Canuto recognized them as glyphs, characters that the ancient Maya used in the first writing system developed anywhere in America.

Mystery upon mystery

Analysis showed that the panel matched the Site Q panels. It was made from the same stone. Its style showed that it was likely carved by one of the Site Q carvers. And the text fit with accounts on the other panels. They told how La Corona had been caught up in a war in the A.D. 670s between two powerful Maya centers, Calakmul and Tikal. At one stage the rulers of La Corona fled to Calakmul when Tikal occupied the city.

Canuto believes that he has found Site Q. But there may be more to come. Canuto's colleague, David A. Freidel of Southern Methodist University in Dallas, Texas, notes that at least one of the Site Q panels seems to have been removed from a throne room. So far, no such room has turned up at La Corona. Solving one mystery has created a new one.

History's detectives

Mysteries are not new to experts who study the ancient Maya. Archaeologists are history's detectives. They use whatever clues they can find to piece together a picture of the past. Like detectives, they use the most up-to-date technology to gather as much information as possible from ruins in

> Cities such as Palenque in Mexico had centers with huge stone palaces and pyramids that were the focus for public rituals. Other buildings were made of wood that has not survived.

∧ A Guatemalan Maya watches a giant kite on the Day of the Dead while another is prepared behind him. The festival has its origins in Maya rituals.

the rain forests, from artifacts, or from human skeletons.

In the second half of the 20th century, archaeologists learned how to read Maya glyphs. Many panels gave details about Maya kings that help us to understand Maya history. But other information is hard to get at. The Maya often rebuilt new monuments on top of old ones, so many of the earliest ruins are buried. To reach them, archaeologists have to tunnel deep beneath the ground. The work is uncomfortable, and even dangerous. The tunnels are no place for anyone who suffers from claustrophobia.

< Many Maya buildings are overgrown or buried beneath later Maya structures, so archaeologists often have to do a lot of digging or tunneling to get to them.

Secrets of the glyphs

When the Spaniards conquered the Maya in the 16th century, they destroyed most Maya books. More importantly, the Maya themselves forgot the meaning of the glyphs used in books or carved on monuments in abandoned cities. When Maya studies began in the 19th century, scholars understood only a few signs connected with the calendar and religious festivals. They assumed that all Maya writing was about similar subjects.

That assumption changed in the second half of the 20th century. In the 1950s, Russian linguist Yuri Knorosov developed a theory that there were two kinds of glyph. Some were pictures that stood for ideas or things. But others represented sounds that could be combined to make different words, like letters or syllables in our alphabet.

Pioneering scholars such as Heinrich Berlin and Tatiana Proskouriakoff showed that Knorosov was basically right. Their findings surprised the experts: It turned out that most Maya texts were historical records of rulers and events. Thanks to the precision of the Maya calendar, their dates could be translated into a day, month, and year in the modern calendar. Later scholars such as

∧ **David Stuart (*right*), Barbara Fash, and two Honduran colleagues sort pieces of stone at Copán to identify glyphs.**

Peter Mathews and David Stuart went on to uncover a detailed history of the Maya, the only Native American culture for which such a complete record exists.

Glyphs are still difficult to read, but archaeologists did have one lucky break. Although the Maya spoke many languages, they had only one language for writing.

Living legacy

Experts in the Maya have another great source of information: The Maya themselves. More than seven million descendants of the ancient Maya still live in the highlands of southern Mexico and Guatemala, Belize, the Yucatán Peninsula, and western El Salvador and Honduras. They still practice traditions archaeologists recognize from ancient carvings. They visit the ruined cities of their ancestors and climb the pyramids for picnics or celebrations. They include ancient rituals in Roman Catholic worship. Some Maya priests still use the ancient 260-day calendar that was created to schedule religious ceremonies.

A wide influence

Evidence of the Maya is scattered over an area of 125,000 square miles (325,000 sq km). Maya cities stood in highlands and lowlands, in rain forests

< Rain forest birds called quetzals decorate this Maya pottery jar from Guatemala.

and on coasts. The Maya were never a united people, however; they did not even speak a single language. Many of their languages were only distantly related to one another. The city-states traded, but they were also rivals, like Calakmul and Tikal.

Disputed dates

Great cities such as Tikal are among the best-known traces of the Maya. Pyramids, temples, and other buildings often stand within the rain forest. The Maya maintained a careful balance between their urban centers and the nearby forest. Sometimes the cities were built in clusters. All of the cities were linked by long-distance trade routes.

Archaeologists once believed that it was only during the so-called Classic period of Maya history, beginning in about A.D. 250, that the Maya cities and society became highly developed. As you'll learn in chapter 2, however, recent discoveries suggest that Maya cities were more developed at a far earlier stage. They may have been inspired by an earlier people from Mesoamerica, the Olmec. The earliest Maya writing is now thought to date from as early as 300 B.C.

Periods of the Maya

Scholars traditionally divide Maya history into three periods: Preclassic, Classic, and Postclassic. Traditionally, the middle period was the highpoint of Maya culture, following a time of development and ending in a long decline. This book uses the traditional periods, because they are a useful shorthand. As you will see in the chapters, however, many archaeologists now question how different the periods really were. Many aspects of Maya culture associated with the Classic period are now known to have begun in the Preclassic. In the same way, some areas of Maya population, such as the cities of the Yucatán in Mexico, only reached their high point in the Postclassic period.

When is a discovery not a discovery?

Most Americans and Europeans only became familiar with the Maya in the mid-19th century. The American writer John Lloyd Stephens and the artist Frederick Catherwood published accounts of their travels to the great Maya cities. Archaeological investigation began in the 1880s, when Alfred Maudslay began clearing sites and making drawings of their layouts.

Such pioneers sometimes get credit for "discovering" the Maya. But for millions of living Maya, their ancestors were never lost. They live among the ruins in the forest, celebrate rituals in ancient plazas, and even eat the same foods as their ancestors. For them, the people of the past are still a part of everyday life.

Archaeologists could help make the Maya more familiar with their past, however. The Maya had lost the ability to read glyphs, for example, before archaeologists interpreted them. Today, Maya archaeologists work alongside other experts to understand the secrets of their history.

> This photograph shows Alfred Maudslay's visit to Palenque in the 1880s. Maudslay may be the man in the tower.

In Chapters 3 and 4 you'll learn about the great cities of the Classic period. They were ruled by sacred kings and inspired by worship of the Maya gods. Their rituals included an unusual form of sacrifice: Kings cut themselves in order to offer their blood to the gods.

A long decline?

Chapter 5 looks at how the Maya lived: What they ate and how they grew their food. They were farmers, but as coastal archaeologists are discovering, they were also skilled traders and navigators. In the last chapter you'll read about the Postclassic period, when the focus of Maya culture shifted to the Yucatán Peninsula of Mexico. The shift was once seen as a sign of a huge collapse in Maya society. As you'll see, however, archaeologists are learning that they may have to change their views. New evidence suggests that Maya society was indeed reorganized—but not that it suffered a catastrophic collapse.

The Coming of the Maya

What was the secret of the hidden paintings?

William Saturno was frustrated. He had wasted two days. It was March 2001, and the archaeologist from the University of New Hampshire was on a visit to Guatemala to study inscriptions at Maya sites. The plans had gotten mixed up, however, and instead he found himself at a site named San Bartolo, which archaeologists knew little about. There was no sign of any inscriptions on its monument. The site was

< Watched by fellow archaeologist William Saturno, Monica Pellecer Alecio removes a stone figure from the oldest known Maya royal tomb, at San Bartolo.

PRECLASSIC
1500 B.C. – A.D. 250

1500 B.C.   0   A.D. 1500

clearly known to looters, however. They had dug tunnels and trenches to hunt for buried treasure.

Shock meeting

Saturno wandered into a tunnel to find some shade. He shone his flashlight on the wall—and found himself looking at the face of the Maya maize (corn) god. Saturno realized that he was looking at the corner of a painted mural—but it took two years of planning to see the rest of the image.

The wall was one of two left from a buried chamber. The Maya had knocked down the other walls to fill in the chamber so that they could build on top. With the help of Guatemalan Humberto Amador, an expert tunneler, Saturno began to remove the rubble. They left a thin layer of soil and rock to protect the face of the wall. Then they called in experts to clear the mural without damaging it.

The mural was 30 feet (9 m) long, which made it hard to see. Saturno had an inspired idea. He held a flatbed scanner up against the wall and made a scan. It worked perfectly. About 350 scans later, Saturno pieced

∧ The Maya maize god as he appears in the mural found by William Saturno at San Bartolo, from the first century B.C.

> This sculpture of the maize god in the shape of a personified maize cob was created nearly 800 years after the mural, in Copán.

∧ **William Saturno (*right*) and Humberto Amador worked 50 feet (15 m) underground for weeks in a small tunnel only 3 to 4 feet (1–1.5 m) wide.**

together a remarkable scene: The Maya creation story. As well as the maize god, the mural featured the coronation of what might have been a real-life king.

Atomic bombshell

Saturno believes that the mural was painted by two artists, with different styles. But when did they work? Saturno used radiocarbon dating to find out. All living things contain the element carbon. Once they die, the atoms of one kind of carbon begin to decay at a regular speed. By measuring how much carbon had decayed from the plant material used to make paint for the mural, Saturno got a good idea of how long ago the plants died.

The results were remarkable. The mural dated from about 100 B.C. Many experts had believed that the Maya did not develop advanced states until later in their history. The mural at San Bartolo showed that the Maya already had clear ideas about royalty and religious beliefs in the first century B.C.

The oldest tomb

There was more to come. In 2005 Saturno's Guatemalan colleague Monica Pellecer Alecio found a sealed tomb beneath a small pyramid about a mile west of the mural chamber. She had to hurry: She had heard that looters were in the area. The team worked around the clock. At about

∧ This artist's re-creation shows laborers building a stepped pyramid at the early city of El Mirador, using limestone blocks held together with mortar.

2:00 A.M. on the third day, they levered open the top of the burial chamber. Inside lay a man's skeleton and a number of artifacts. On the man's chest was a plaque made of jade—a symbol of Maya royalty.

The bones in the tomb dated from about 150 B.C. Radiocarbon dating is not exact, so there is a chance that the buried king was the man from the mural—or perhaps his father.

Writing from prehistory

San Bartolo may not be done with its revelations. In 2005, another of Saturno's colleagues, Boris Beltrán, found a painting that included glyphs. Dating back to about 300 B.C., it is the earliest Maya writing known so far. It is so old that archaeologists have not yet learned how to read it. The rest of the site has 140 buildings covering about 0.4 square mile (1 sq km), including ball courts and monuments. Saturno believes that the site was built in about 400 B.C. Evidence suggests that it was abandoned in about A.D. 100—but later reoccupied beginning in about A.D. 600.

Gods and heroes

The maize god was prominent on the San Bartolo murals for a good reason. Maize was the staple food of the Maya. It was essential to their survival, just as it is for Maya farmers today. More evidence of the importance of the god came in 2004 at a site in Guatemala named Cival. A team led by Francisco Estrada-Belli, of Vanderbilt University, in Nashville,

Tennessee, found two giant stone faces positioned on either side of a stairway that climbed a pyramid. The eyes are decorated with what may be husks of corn. The archaeologist believes that the faces represent the maize god.

A large site

Estrada-Belli used photographs from satellites to get an overview of Cival. He learned that it was about twice as large as it looked from the ground. By 500 B.C., the town had been home to about 10,000 people. The photographs also revealed that the central plaza was built so that it faced the rising sun. Offerings had been left in the plaza for the gods, including jars, a red bowl, and polished jade pebbles.

Estrada-Belli believes that the plaza was used for rituals to celebrate the endless cycle of maize, the vital

Models for the Maya

The Maya were not the first civilization to emerge in Mesoamerica. Archaeologists working on Mexico's Gulf Coast found huge stone heads and the remains of cities. In the 1950s, scientists used radiocarbon dating to find out when the cities were built. One site, San Lorenzo, dated from about 1200 B.C.—far earlier than any other city in the Americas. Its builders are known as the Olmec. The Olmec introduced many elements that were shared by later civilizations in the region, including the Maya: Pyramids, ball courts, altars, memorial stones called stelae, calendars, and maize and rain gods. The influence of the Olmec likely spread through trade: Merchants carried Olmec artifacts—and Olmec ideas—over the whole region.

crop which grew, died, and was reborn each year. Rituals may also have welcomed new rulers to the throne. Estrada-Belli discovered a stone slab that featured one of the earliest known images of a Maya king.

Yet again, a discovery suggested that Maya society was well developed much earlier than experts once thought, with kings, rituals, and complex symbols used in art. Perhaps the Preclassic period wasn't so very different from the Classic after all.

◁ In this artist's reconstruction, a scribe chisels glyphs into a limestone slab. Such monuments, called stelae, were erected in Maya cities to record the reigns and achievements of kings and other historical events.

Cities in the Forest

When did the Maya build their urban centers?

Robert J. Sharer, an archaeologist from the University of Pennsylvania, turned cameraman to film his colleague Jane Buikstra. Sharer had invited the University of New Mexico expert to Copán, a site in western Honduras, to examine human remains he had found in a Maya tomb. The rich clothes and jade objects with the body suggested that this was a royal burial: a Maya king. The camera rolled while Buikstra described the bones that lay on a stone slab.

< Each 2 feet (60 cm) high, these ceramic figures once stood outside the tomb of a royal scribe in Copán. They may represent former rulers of the city.

PRECLASSIC 1500 B.C. – A.D. 250

CLASSIC A.D. 250 – 900

1500 B.C.   0   A.D. 1500

∧ The remains beneath Margarita were dyed red from a mineral used to paint the body.

< Excavators wore protective clothing until the tomb was declared free of harmful chemicals.

Buikstra estimated that the king had been over 50 years old when he died. The bones were unusually bright and reddish. The color was created by a substance called cinnabar, a red mineral that the Maya believed was sacred. They had coated the body with cinnabar before burial.

Then Sharer asked Buikstra to confirm what sex the person had been. It was a routine question: Both of them assumed that the body was male—and both were in for a huge shock. The female pelvis is lighter and smaller than the male pelvis, to make childbirth easier. The pelvis in the tomb left no doubt: The "king" had been a queen.

Getting to the bottom of it

The tomb lay in a structure now named Margarita. There are so many ruins at Copán that archaeologists use nicknames to identify them more easily. Margarita stood at the bottom of a mound known as the Acropolis. The Acropolis is not a single structure but a whole series of monuments built one on top of the other.

The oldest structures are at the very bottom of Maya ruins. That usually makes them difficult to investigate. But archaeologists at Copán had a stroke of luck. Sometime in the past, a river changed course and ate away part of the Acropolis, carving a 100-foot (30-m) slice through the mound. By tunneling near the bottom of the cliff face left by the river, archaeologists were able to start exploring the oldest parts of the Acropolis first.

Names of a dynasty

Sharer and his team had another lucky break. Glyphs at Copán provide the fullest history of a city's kings anywhere in the Maya world. An artifact known as Altar Q is carved with images of 16 rulers—the line of

∧ **Archaeologist William Saturno (*left*) surveys a mound near Copán that may contain evidence about how people lived in the city's suburbs.**

kings who ruled Copán beginning in the early 400s. Sharer believes that the dead queen may have been the queen mother of a whole dynasty.

If that were the case, she was the wife of the founder of the line, K'inich Yax K'uk' Mo' (Sun-eyed Green Quetzal Macaw). Although his wife's name is not known, the king's name turns up everywhere in Copán. No later kings were celebrated as much.

All the clues pointed to the fact that the king was buried somewhere near Margarita in the heart of the Acropolis. Altar Q stood there, along with an elaborate monument named the Rosalila and the tomb of the queen. There was even a stone carved with glyphs that referred to the "death house of the lord of Copán."

In 1997, archaeologists tunneling into the Acropolis found another royal tomb 50 feet (15 m) beneath the grassy surface above. This time the skeleton was male. It was buried with a jade pectoral—a chest ornament—that was shown being worn by K'inich Yax K'uk' Mo' in the carving on Altar Q. The skeleton's right arm was badly disfigured. Perhaps, archaeologists wonder, that was why the founder was shown on Altar Q with his right arm hidden behind his shield.

V This artist's reconstruction shows the Rosalila both as it originally appeared and in position today, buried beneath the Acropolis.

Center of influence

Copán stood at the western edge of the Maya world, in what is now western Honduras. It was far from great centers such as Tikal, but it ruled a kingdom of about 20,000 people. Signs suggest that K'inich Yax K'uk' Mo' introduced Copán to influences from the city of Teotihuacan, 700 miles (1,125 km) away in central Mexico. With about 125,000 inhabitants, Teotihuacan was, until it was deserted in about A.D. 600, the largest city anywhere in the Americas. The king's tomb contained a carving of a pyramid temple like those in the other city.

Signs of Teotihuacan's influence are found in most Maya capitals. Some

Artistic reconstruction

The reconstruction of the Rosalila on the opposite page is the work of artist Chris Klein, of the National Geographic Society. Klein has been studying Copán since 1991, when he first visited the site to paint the Rosalila soon after its discovery. Because the monument was buried beneath later structures, and difficult to photograph in its entirety, artwork would be able to reveal a fuller picture: But only if it was absolutely precise.

In order to understand how the Rosalila was laid out, Klein had to work underground. He crawled through tunnels so hot that his hands got damp and kept slipping on his pencils. He checked every stage with archaeologists. And Klein went back to Copán again and again to make sure that his images reflected the very latest discoveries. The results are reconstructions so precise that they have in turn become a valuable tool for the archaeologists trying to re-create an image of ancient Copán.

∧ Klein (*center*) discusses an illustration with his colleagues.

carvings show figures with eyes like goggles (as on page 27). They resemble Teotihuan portraits of the god Tlaloc. Blades made from a hard volcanic rock called obsidian probably came from within Teotihuacan territory: The stone does not occur in Maya territory.

Tales of Tikal

For years, scholars have debated whether the influence of Teotihuacan spread through peaceful contact such as trade or through invasions of Maya territory. No one knows for sure.

A clue may lie almost 200 miles (320 km) from Copán, in the lowlands of northern Guatemala known as the Petén. In the Early Classic period, the region was the focus of Maya city building. Among the urban centers that grew there was one of the most powerful Maya capitals: Tikal.

Excavations at Tikal by the University of Pennsylvania began in 1956 and lasted for 15 years. More than 100 archaeologists flew in to the rain forest, where they landed on a runway built by the Guatemalan army. The excavations uncovered more than 500 buildings on a site that covered 25 square miles (65 sq km) and had been home to 45,000 people.

The excavations enabled experts to put together a timeline for the city. It began as a farming village before 600 B.C. Five hundred years later, a group of monuments now called the North Acropolis were being used for burials. Archaeologists found that skeletons there were taller and stronger than those of most Maya. That suggests a noble class had emerged, whose diet was better than that of most people.

By the 2nd century A.D., Tikal had become a major center. One of the oldest Maya stelae that includes a date glyph confirms that inhabitants of Tikal were writing by A.D. 292. The stela celebrated the crowning of a new ruler. It is often taken as marking the start of the Classic period.

A story in stones

Archaeologist David Stuart believes that glyphs from Tikal contain evidence of an invasion by warriors from Teotihuacan. In 378, Stuart believes, a man named Fire Is Born "arrived from the west." On the very same day Jaguar Paw, the ruler of Tikal, died. Stuart interprets the story as describing the arrival of a general

▼ The plaza at the heart of Tikal was dominated by two 140-foot-tall (43 m) temple pyramids, built by the ruler Ah Cacaw in the A.D. 680s.

from Teotihuacan, who killed the Tikal king. In his reading, the general then put his lord's son on the throne of Tikal. The new ruler, Nun Yax Ayin, is shown on a stela with weapons and goggles in Teotihuacan style. He was the founder of a new, foreign dynasty.

Mighty Tikal

Stuart's theory is just that: A theory. Reading the glyphs is notoriously tricky. Not everyone accepts Stuart's ideas. Some believe that Fire Is Born should be called Smoking Frog, for example.

∧ Expert John Keshishian makes a rubbing of a stela from Tikal. A rubbing shows up the raised surfaces of glyphs, making them easier to read.

Whatever happened, Tikal continued to grow. It may have been helped by links with Teotihuacan, either through trade or by military power. Its rulers became overlords of nearby cities.

Then, in 562, Tikal suffered a military defeat and was thrown into chaos. Other cities also seem to have experienced a crisis. Teotihuacan itself was overthrown by unidentified attackers and abandoned. For Tikal, however, power would return. In the Late Classic period of the late 7th century, its temples were built even higher than before until they towered over the rain forests surrounding them.

Kings, Gods, and Sacrifice

CHAPTER 4

How did kings link the Maya with their gods?

By July 1952, Mexican archaeologist Alberto Ruz had been excavating at the Maya city of Palenque for three years—and all he had to show for it was 73 feet (22 m) of steep stairs leading deep inside a pyramid. Ruz had been clearing a temple full of carved glyphs when he noticed its unusual floor. Most temple floors were covered with a layer of plaster called stucco. This one had a floor of flagstones, including one drilled with two rows of holes that had been filled with stone plugs.

< Alberto Ruz discovered a stone staircase that led deep into the pyramid beneath the Temple of Inscriptions in Palenque.

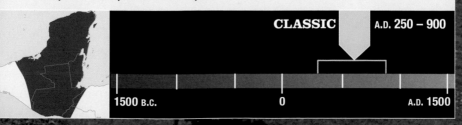

	CLASSIC	A.D. 250 – 900

1500 B.C.	0	A.D. 1500

< The stairway beneath the pyramid uses arches called corbels, which are common in Maya buildings.

found the top of a stairway. In great heat and humidity, Ruz and his men starting clearing the rubble, breaking up large rocks to move them. The air was thick with dust and the work was slow. By the end of the first season they had revealed only 23 steps.

Hide and seek

Four seasons—and 600,000 pounds (270,000 kg) of rubble—later, Ruz finally reached the bottom of the stairs. He felt that he was on to something. Hot: Ruz broke through a wall into a small room that held jade, ceramics, and other offerings to the gods. Hotter still: Ruz and his men broke down a second 12-foot-thick (3.5-m) wall into another chamber. It held a stone chest that contained the skeletons of five or six people in their late teens. To Ruz, it seemed clear that they had been sacrificed. But why? He thought that they might have been killed to guard a king in the afterlife.

Like other researchers before him, Ruiz had no idea what the stone was for. Then, one morning, he had a breakthrough. On his hands and knees he examined the joint between the floor and the walls—and realized that the walls continued down out of sight. There must be another room beneath the floor. Ruz got his team to lift the unusual slab—but only an opening full of rubble was revealed.

Clearing the steps

Ruz's flash of inspiration began four years of hard work. When he cleared away some stones, he saw that he had

Boiling hot: One of the diggers felt his crowbar pass through the last wall and into empty space. Ruz took a flashlight and peered through the

Pacal's jade funeral mask was one of many Maya artifacts stolen from a Mexican museum in 1985, but retrieved four years later.

Alberto Ruz shows visitors the lid of Pacal's tomb, carved with an image of the ruler falling into the underworld.

opening. He later wrote, "Out of the shadows emerged a vision from a fairy tale."

Into the tomb

Ruz was the first person for 1,300 years to look inside the royal tomb of Palenque. The walls sparkled as if with ice—the effect was caused by the lime with which they had been painted—and the floor was a slab of carved stone. When he managed to get into the chamber a couple of days later, Ruz drilled a hole in the slab and saw that it was not a floor but a lid. The lid covered a massive stone sarcophagus that held human bones and a wealth of precious objects. Hundreds were made from jade, a material linked to royalty.

Years later, experts in reading glyphs announced that the remains were those of a great king, Lord Pacal, who reigned in Palenque between A.D. 615 and 683.

The Late Classic

It was an astonishing find. Not only did the tomb contain many precious artifacts. It was one of the first to be found within a Maya pyramid. The pyramid was raised to honor Pacal, and he had built other monuments—a palace and at least three temples—to his own glory. Later finds at other sites confirmed that other kings were buried beneath their own pyramids. These monarchs were not just kings: They were links to the gods. Carvings and paintings show kings and queens

∧ **This carved relief from El Tajin in Mexico shows a man being sacrificed after playing a ball game that was sacred to the Maya.**

cutting themselves or piercing their tongues to sacrifice their blood to the gods. Royalty was essential to the rituals that kept the gods happy and ensured the well-being of the people.

Kings and lords

Religion was at the heart of Maya life. It inspired astronomers to study the movement of bodies in the night sky. Astronomy and religion also underlay the two Maya calendars. One was based on a 260-day cycle, the second on 365 days. Every 52 years—using modern years—both calendars ended on the same day. This momentous event was believed to mark the start of a new cycle. In the Early Classic, a third calendar was introduced for recording the enthronement, marriages, and deaths of kings.

Deadly games

The ball courts found in Maya cities were also closely associated with ritual and sacrifice. The sunken courts were shaped like a capital I and lined by seats for spectators. Statues and paintings show that players wore protective belts and knee and elbow pads. The large rubber ball could be hit with the hips, knees, or elbows—but not the hands. The scoring system

Rescue of an ancient king

In October 2001 rain washed away mud to expose an altar on a ball court at Cancuén, Guatemala. Carvings on the stone showed the king of Cancuén playing the ball game against another local ruler, perhaps to celebrate an alliance. The altar was found by looters, who took it and tried to sell it. When drug runners made a violent attempt to grab the altar from the gang, anxious villagers appealed to Arthur Demarest, an archaeologist from Vanderbilt University,

Tennessee, who was working in the area. He contacted the authorities and in April 2003 armed police raided the gang's hideout. They captured the leader—but the altar had been sold. The dealer who now had the altar got scared. He buried it near Cancuén to wait until it was safe to sell. Acting on tip-offs, undercover police got the altar back in October 2003.

V **The year after the altar was recovered, this identical altar was found at Cancuén.**

Sacrifice or execution?

The Maya made offerings to their gods—including human sacrifices. Some scholars, however, believe that the idea of sacrifice does not help us to understand Maya beliefs, because it makes them seem cruel. They argue that many Maya sacrifices were enemies captured in battle. Their deaths were an extension of the killing that is inevitable in all warfare: They simply took place in sacred places rather than on the battlefield. Scholars also argue that Maya nobles sacrificed their own blood, including piercing their skin with the spines of stingrays. It may be that the Maya saw being given to the gods as an honor, rather than a punishment—although their victims may have disagreed.

∨ **This scene from Bonampak shows city nobles killing captives. Human sacrifice was important to the Maya, but it rarely took place on such a scale as in the great cities of the neighboring Aztec.**

is not clear, but it may have involved hitting the ball through stone rings found on the sides of some courts.

The ball game had a highly important ritual meaning. In a Maya myth, two characters named the Hero Twins play the game and defeat the gods of the Underworld. In the real game, it seems that the losers may have been sacrificed. Some archaeologists, however, argue that perhaps it was the winners who had the honor of sacrificing their lives.

Great paintings

The Lacandon Indians of the Mexican state of Chiapas still prayed amid the ruins of their Maya ancestors in the mid–20th century. When American Giles Healey visited them to make a documentary in 1946, the Lacandon

Mary's mural makeover

The murals at Bonampak are well preserved, but they have still suffered over the centuries. Today, even the moisture in the breath of tourists visiting the site threatens to damage the paint. When the murals were first discovered, they were photographed and reproduced by two different artists. In the mid-1980s, however, the Mexican government had the murals cleaned, allowing a closer look at the paintings, this time using cutting-edge technology.

Leading Maya art expert Mary Miller has used computer enhancement to study the murals. First she scanned photographs of the murals into a computer before she and artist Douglas Stern journeyed to Bonampak. Using transparent acetate, Stern carefully copied the murals, recording details that did not show up in the photographs. Stern's work was fed into the computer. More data came from infrared photos that revealed details invisible to the naked eye.

Miller also worked on the faded colors of the murals. Analysis of the paint used by the Bonampak artists revealed what the colors would have looked like when fresh. The colors were also added to the computer images. Miller was able to produce beautiful, enhanced versions of the murals that are not guesswork but triumphs of scientific reconstruction.

∧ **Mary Miller and Douglas Stern compare a copy of a mural with its on-screen version.**

offered to show him a site named Bonampak. There, in a three-roomed stone structure that had mostly been overlooked by earlier visitors, Healey was astonished to see the walls covered with bright paintings. They had been preserved by a lucky accident: Rain leaking through the plaster ceiling had covered them with a layer of calcium carbonate that protected them but through which they could still be seen.

The Bonampak murals date from A.D. 791. They record a real occasion when a king presented his son to the people as his successor. The murals showed scenes of war, bloodletting, and sacrifice. That made scholars in the 1940s reconsider their belief that the Maya were largely peaceable farmers. But the murals also gave a glimpse of the bright costumes, and constant music and dancing that must have filled a Maya court. In the hundreds of colorful figures, the murals at Bonampak are our most vivid record yet of the Maya as they saw themselves.

The Past in the Present

CHAPTER 5

How was Maya life like life today?

Archaeologists can pick up information from all kinds of sources—even dirty dishes. In 2002, Terry Powis, an archaeologist at the University of Texas, began to examine pots found at the Maya city of Colha. There were fourteen, all with spouts for pouring. But what had they held? Powis scraped out the dry remains from the pots and sent them for chemical analysis. The results? Three of the pots had contained a drink made from chocolate.

< Many parts of Maya life survive today, from these traditional designs being embroidered by a Maya woman from Chiapas, Mexico, to a taste for chocolate.

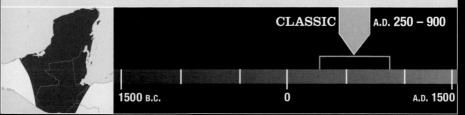

CLASSIC   A.D. 250 – 900

1500 B.C.   0   A.D. 1500

Archaeologists already knew from murals and paintings on ceramics that the Maya liked chocolate. Made from the roasted and ground beans of the cacao tree, it was immensely popular with both rich and poor.

What was surprising about the Colha pots was their date: About 500 B.C. That was a thousand years earlier than any previous evidence of chocolate drinking. That suggested that chocolate was discovered before the Maya, perhaps by a people such as the Olmec. The drink became a favorite in all Mesoamerican cultures—just as it is a favorite today.

> This ceramic jar shows a goddess as a cacao tree, the source of beans for chocolate.

V The cacao tree produces pods (red) that contain the beans that are roasted to produce chocolate.

Sweet and sour

You'd probably be surprised if you tried Maya chocolate. It tastes quite bitter. The ancient Maya sweetened it with honey or mixed it with water. They even added maize or chili to it. They liked to drink it with a thick froth on top. They created the froth by pouring the drink from a height or possibly by blowing into the spout of the pot to mix air with the drink.

∧ Fires burn as farmers clear land for planting in the Yucatán in Mexico. Ash from the fires is a good fertilizer, but the soil soon loses its nutrients.

Farming the forest

Even in the heart of the rain forest, Maya life depended on farming—but not always in fields. Maya farmers managed the forest. They weeded the forest floor or cleared trees to help food plants grow. The forest was also home to animals that were hunted for food, such as deer, armadillos, and birds. The Maya raised no animals except dogs, ducks, and turkeys, which were all eaten.

Another major source of food was rivers or, near the coasts, the sea. Bones and piles of empty shells at Maya sites show that fish and shellfish were a large part of the diet. From the early Preclassic period, Maya sailors went out to sea in search of fish.

The chief Maya crop was maize. If the maize harvest failed, a community was in danger of starving. Their diet also included other plants, such as beans, squash, chilis, and avocados.

Archaeologists do not fully understand Maya farming methods. Soils in the region have poor nutrients for crops. The present-day Maya use a technique known as slash-and-burn. A farmer cuts down an area of forest and sets the felled brushwood on fire. Then he plants his seeds in the ash, which fertilizes the soil. With enough rain, the land will yield a good harvest for a few seasons. Then it is left to recover. The farmer clears more forest and starts the process again.

The Maya at the movies

In 2006, Hollywood star Mel Gibson directed the movie *Apocalypto*, which was set during the decline of the Maya in the 7th century. Although Gibson's advisers made sure that the characters wore clothing and jewelry based on that of the ancient Maya, many archaeologists and modern Maya accused the movie of inaccuracy. It portrayed forest Maya as hunters living in idyllic isolation, for example. In fact, most Maya were farmers who worked hard and who were linked to the urban centers by trade. The movie showed the ruler of a Maya city as a cruel king making large-scale human sacrifices—a practice that experts point out is more closely linked with the Aztec. In reality, Maya kings played a complex role as cultural and religious leaders for their communities. Overall, archaeologists and Maya were disappointed that the movie seemed to suggest that the Maya were a savage, violent people, rather than outstanding mathematicians, astronomers, craftworkers, architects, traders, and artists.

⋀ Most experts argued that *Apocalypto* gave an inaccurate picture of Maya life.

Enough for everyone

The Maya seem to have practiced slash-and-burn agriculture throughout their history. But their cities grew so large that slash-and-burn farming alone would not have grown enough food to feed the population. Farmers had to find other ways to increase production. One way was to build terraces, or flat steps, in hillsides. The terraces both provided more land for crops and helped to prevent rain from washing soil off the hillside.

Evidence of another form of farming came in the 1960s. A Canadian geographer named Alfred Siemens used aerial photographs to study the southwestern Yucatán in Mexico.

Photographs taken from airplanes often reveal patterns in the landscape that are hard to see from the ground.

A telltale mosaic

Along a swampy river valley, Siemens could see a regular pattern of humps, like a mosaic. Field trips to the area confirmed Siemens's hunch: The humps were artificial. The Maya had turned swamp into farmland by digging channels and piling up the rich soil to create raised fields.

How much raised-field farming the Maya carried out is not clear, but in the 1970s and 1980s a technique called synthetic-aperture radar provided part of the answer. The airborne instrument can see through the vegetation of the rain forest to map features on the ground. Among the forests of southern Mexico and Guatemala, the radar showed what some experts think was a huge area of fields. Other archaeologists argue that the features may be largely natural. No one knows for sure.

In dry areas such as the Yucatán coast, the Maya used irrigation for farming and to supply water to cities. At Edzná, researchers from Brigham Young University in Provo, Utah, found canals and reservoirs that made sure the city had enough water. One canal was a remarkable 100 yards (92 m) wide and 7 miles (115 km) long.

Homes in history

People's homes reflected their position in society. Kings and nobles lived in stone palaces. The palaces and other ceremonial buildings in the cities needed laborers to build them and specialists such as scribes and priests to maintain them. Such people lived in stone houses, which sometimes served as workshops. Outside the city, farmers lived in round homes with walls of adobe— mud bricks dried in the sun—and roofs of thatch. Many modern Maya live in similar homes today.

< This ancient Maya figure shows a woman weaving. Maya women still make cloth in exactly the same way today.

Maritime masters

Few people think of the Maya as great sailors, but archaeologists have recently investigated Maya seafaring. As late as the 16th century, written records show, Maya merchants were making long voyages west to Aztec Mexico and as far south as Panama. Their canoes were 80 feet (25 m) long and packed with cargo. In the 1980s, Anthony Andrews of the New College of Florida excavated Isla Cerritos on the north coast of the Yucatán, which served as a port for the city of Chichén Itzá. He revealed that the port had extensive trade links. Other archaeologists have explored the more substantial remains of Tulum, a port on the east coast that benefited from a natural water supply and a harbor that was protected by a coral reef. These and other Maya ports prospered for centuries, down to and even for a time after the Spanish conquest.

∧ A canoe laden with cargo is guided by signal fires to the port of Tulum on the coast of the Yucatán in this artist's rendition.

Trade tricks

Artifacts found all over Mesoamerica show that the Maya were part of a large trading network. Merchants carried goods along tracks, down rivers, and around the coasts.

Much of the trade took place among groups of Maya. Fish and salt from the coast were exchanged for farm produce from inland. The southern highlands exported cacao beans to make chocolate, basalt to make grinding stones for maize, flints to use to spark fire, and obsidian, which could be worked to produce razor-sharp knife edges.

material came. Luxury items from the coast included conch shells, which were used as trumpets, and stingray spines used in bloodletting rituals. Such items show that the Maya had become skilled at using the resources of the coral reefs that lay just off the coast of the Yucatán.

From the forest came the green feathers of the quetzal, a key part of royal costume. Later, when the Aztecs had become the dominant power in central Mexico, the Maya exported quetzal feathers, jade, and cacao beans to them. Maya imports were luxury goods in the Aztec cities. In return, the Maya received artifacts made from copper, which was the first metal known to their culture.

∧ The green feathers of the quetzal were a symbol of royalty. The Maya traded them throughout Mexico.

A luxury market

The Maya elite created a demand for luxuries. Jade, the symbol of kingship, was found in large quantities in only one place, the Motagua River valley in the highlands of Guatemala. It was carved by skilled craft workers in the lowlands, then taken all over Maya territory, including back to the highlands from which the raw

∧ Jade was carved into figures such as this one, but was also used for jewelry for royalty.

Meet an Archaeologist

William Saturno is assistant professor of archaeology at Boston University. In 2001, he discovered the oldest-known Maya murals at San Bartolo in Guatemala. Since then, he has directed fieldwork at the site.

What made you want to be an archaeologist?
As a child I loved dirt. I used to dig in my backyard, using spoons from the kitchen. I never found much, usually just the twisted spoons from earlier excavation attempts, but as far as I was concerned I was an archaeologist. I guess it was just the mystery of it. I loved going to the museum, seeing mummies and the like. My mother said that I used to say I liked the way it smelled.

How did you get interested in the Maya?
It was somewhat of an accident. My main interest was Egypt and Iraq, but I got the chance to work in Mexico and I visited Palenque. It was the most fascinating place I had ever seen. Not long after that, the Gulf War broke out and I saw it would be a long time before I would ever get to dig in Iraq, so Mesoamerica and eventually the Maya area became my home.

What's the best part of your job?
The best part of my job is discovery; it doesn't matter if it is big or small, breathtaking or seemingly insignificant, just being able to find the remnants from the past and put them together to see how the Maya lived, thrived, struggled in their society. There isn't anything else I would rather do.

What qualities does an archaeologist need?
Archaeologists have to have great memories. Much of what we do is about comparing one artifact to another, remembering something we saw in a museum collection years ago, remembering a glyph or a pot fragment. You need memory to recognize patterns, and patterns are vital to interpreting what we find.

Do you have any advice for young people who want to become archaeologists?
My advice is study hard, read everything you can get your hands on, and get as much exposure to other cultures as you can. That and

learn how to dig with a trowel.

Q Is there much left to learn about the Maya?
A Despite all of our efforts and more than 100 years of digging, there is much we don't know. For example, when I discovered the murals at San Bartolo, they were a complete surprise. No one really anticipated that such a work of art would be found or even would have existed in the 1st century B.C. There are hundreds of Maya sites still left to excavate. All of them have something unexpected to tell us about the Maya.

Q How did you learn to dig tunnels?
A Tunneling is hard and a bit dangerous. I was very lucky to have seen experienced archaeologists tunnel while I was a graduate student working in Copán, Honduras. Saying that, so long as you pay very close attention to what the tunnel is trying to tell you, it sort of digs itself. It tells you which rocks you can move safely and which ones you can't, and you learn as you go.

Q Is it easy to read glyphs?
A Glyphs aren't as hard as they might seem at first glance. Though the signs seem complex, when you practice drawing them they become more familiar.

∧ **William Saturno shows one of his sons scans of the murals at San Bartolo on an on-site computer.**

Q What question would you most like to answer about the ancient Maya?
A I am interested in their origins. I want to understand how the Maya went from being rural farmers to being city-builders. What brought about those changes, who built the first temple pyramid, who was the first to be crowned king?

Q Are the modern Maya like the ancient Maya?
A They share similarities but also exhibit differences. It is sort of like asking if you are like your great-grandfather. You may look a bit like him, you may speak the same language as him, but you probably live in a different

town—and I'm sure he didn't have an iPod.

Q Do your children like being on-site at excavations?
A It is their favorite place in the world. My oldest son talks about being an archaeologist, but he prefers ancient Egypt and Persia to the Maya. My middle son is more interested in animals that live around the ruins than the ruins themselves, and my youngest will make his first journey into the field this spring.

Q Why did the Maya leave their cities in about A.D. 900?
A The Maya left their great lowland cities because those cites no longer provided the lives they wanted.

Survival in the Yucatán

CHAPTER 6

What happened when the Classic period ended?

Alejandro Terrazas can make bones reveal their secrets. In 2003, the archaeologist from Mexico's National Institute of Anthropology and History (NIAH) examined a skeleton found on the floor of a flooded cave in the northern Yucatán Peninsula and began to get a picture of its owner. The bones had belonged to a large man who was far older than most Maya, maybe as old as age 50. He suffered from such bad arthritis that he could barely move his fingers. And his teeth were so rotten than it would have been difficult for him to chew his food.

< An archaeologist diver uses a flashlight to explore the walls of a cenote, or underwater cavern, in the Yucatán.

∧ A diver is lowered by chairlift as archaeologists prepare to dive in a cenote illuminated by powerful underwater lights.

Terrazas was part of an NIAH team carrying out a survey of a whole network of flooded caves. Beneath the surface, the Yucatán is as hollow as an old log. All over the region, small openings in the ground lead into huge underground chambers.

Caves for sacrifice

The Spanish word for the caves is cenotes (say-NO-tays), based on a Maya word meaning *abyss*. The caverns were water sources for Maya towns and villages. They were more than just wells, however. For the Maya, they were also entries to the underworld. The Spaniards who visited the Maya in the early 16th century reported that precious objects were thrown into the cenotes—along with human sacrifices. They were offerings for the rain god Chac, who was thought to live deep within the caves.

Underwater graves

Now Terrazas had new evidence. It came not from the bones, but from how they had been found in the sand. The man had not been thrown into the

Cave-diving scholars

The cenotes of Yucatán are tough to explore. Divers have to squeeze through tiny gaps between caverns. The water is cold and dark: Most divers carry at least three flashlights, just to be safe. The entrances to the caverns are often high above the water; divers use winches to lower their gear—and themselves. And much of the system is too deep to explore using scuba gear. It was only in about 2000, some 25 years after the NIAH introduced underwater archaeology, that archaeologists became skilled enough at cave diving to survey Yucatan's cenotes. There are hundreds scattered in a 110-mile (178-km) circle formed when rain hollowed out cracks in the rock left by a giant meteorite that hit the area 65 million years ago. The archaeologists are racing against time. Every year some 10,000 sport divers explore the cenotes. Every time one disturbs Maya remains, some clues to the past are lost—forever.

water. His body had been placed there after his death. Nearby, another body had been laid on the cave floor with ceramic pots containing offerings to the gods. Clearly, the Maya had not only used cenotes for live sacrifices, but also to dispose of dead bodies.

A change of centers

One reason archaeologists are very interested in the Yucatán is that, starting in the ninth century, it was the center of Maya civilization for 700 years. In the great cities of the Classic period, such as Tikal and Copán, experts have found no buildings dating from after about A.D. 800. All building seems to have stopped. Within a century, the cities were abandoned.

No one knows why the Maya left. Archaeologists have suggested that

drought or harvest failures caused a crisis that sparked wars between city-states over scarce food. Some sites have signs of warfare—but not enough everywhere to support the idea of a general collapse. Some Maya simply seem to have decided to move.

Modern experts tend to reject the idea that there was a clear break between the Classic and Postclassic periods. Instead they stress that the centers of Maya power continued to shift. For a century, cities grew close

< Archaeologist Arturo Gonzalez places a grid over human bones in a cenote. The squares make it easier to record the exact position of each bone.

△ Tourists climb the Pyramid of the Magician in Uxmal. In ancient times, only rulers and priests could climb the steps: The city's population watched rituals from the ground.

together in the fertile Puuc hills of the western Yucatán: Uxmal, Kabah, and Sayil. They were abandoned in their turn. This time the explanation may lie in the physical record.

Mighty Chichén

For about 200 years, the most powerful city in Mesoamerica was Chichén (now called Chichén Itzá) in the northeastern Yucatán. Experts have found evidence at the site that does not occur in earlier Maya cities. There are temples dedicated to the god Quetzalcoatl, the "Feathered Serpent,"

and distinctive statues of figures lying on their backs. There are also reliefs of warriors wearing a new kind of clothing. Offerings in the Sacred Well, a cenote next to the city, contained gold and copper from central Mexico. Such evidence suggests that the Maya had fallen under the influence of the Toltec of central Mexico. Experts call this process "Mexicanization."

Why Chichén declined remains a mystery. Archaeologists are not even sure when it happened. Estimates range from the late 900s to the early 1200s. The Postclassic was a period when many Maya peoples seem to have been moving around, and it is difficult to be able to put together an accurate sequence of events. Perhaps the Itzá simply moved on. In about 1270, for example, they built a city at Mayapán. Again, excavations reveal that the settlement had a complex history. It was occupied and abandoned a number of times before it was finally abandoned in the 1440s.

Other sites reveal a more complete record of occupation. In particular, ports became wealthy thanks to the growth of shipping around the coasts. Inland, sites such as Lamanai, in Belize, were constantly occupied. Experts are hoping that Lamanai may provide a series of radiocarbon samples that may help to finally pin down some of the dates of the Postclassic.

The conquest

In 1528 invaders arrived in the Yucatán—the Spaniards. They overcame Maya resistance with warfare and by the 1540s controlled most of their territory. The Spaniards destroyed Maya artifacts and forced the Maya to become Christians. They enslaved them as laborers. Many Maya died from European diseases against which they had no immunity.

Despite centuries of domination by other peoples, the Maya survived. Maya cities continued to trade, even with the Spaniards. Maya traditions survived, too. Worshipers combined ancient beliefs and festivals with their new Christian faith, for example. For today's Maya, the past is not just for archaeologists: It is a part of everyday life.

∧ The snarling head of Kukulcan guards the Temple of the Warriors in Chichén Itzá. The Maya god resembles both a Toltec god and the Aztec god Quetzalcoatl, the Feathered Serpent.

The Years Ahead

Since the arrival of the Spaniards in the 16th century, most Maya have been poor farmers. Recently, however, their population has increased to over seven million. Most live in Guatemala, where they form the majority of the population, and in Mexico. In both countries, the Maya lack political power and their culture is endangered.

Leading the struggle for equality are Maya scholars, who now play a key role in studying and recording their own culture. They help make the world aware that the Maya are a living people as well as one of the great civilizations of the past.

Archaeologists work with the Maya to protect their heritage. Much is under threat. Ancient cities are in danger from looters, who can sell Maya objects for high prices. Money from tourism helps the Maya in some places, but visitors may accidentally endanger sites. Divers, for example, disturb the Yucatán cenotes. Slash-and-burn farmers, illegal loggers, cattle barons, and drug dealers all threaten old sites. Some farmers and loggers operate within national parks, for example, which are meant to protect historic places.

Many non-Maya archaeologists have helped to form action groups, pressing governments for better protection and conservation of monuments. As in other parts of the world, however, there are many obstacles to progress. The eventual outcome of the fight to preserve the Maya past is far from certain.

∧ The living Maya: A Lacandon Indian and her daughter from Chiapas, Mexico. Numbers are rising, but only about 1,000 Lacandon survive.

Glossary

acropolis – a raised area in the center of a city

artifact – any object changed by human activity

astronomer – someone who studies the movement of heavenly bodies, such as the moon, sun, planets, and stars

ball game – a ritual game played by many Mesoamerican peoples; the exact rules of the game are unclear

black market – the name given to buying and selling illegal goods

ceramics – objects made from clay and fired at high temperatures

circa – about; used to indicate a date that is approximate, and abbreviated as ca

city-state – an area ruled over by a city

domesticated – animals that are used to living close to humans, such as livestock or pets

dynasty – a series of rulers that all come from the same family

economy – the system by which a country creates wealth through making and trading products

empire – a large area in which different territories or peoples are ruled by an emperor

excavation – an archaeological dig

global positioning – technology that uses satellites circling Earth in space to pinpoint locations on Earth's surface

glyph – a carved symbol or picture that the Maya used for writing

inscriptions – words that are carved or engraved into a hard material

irrigation – using water to enable crops to grow in otherwise dry areas

jade – a green semiprecious stone that can be polished to a high shine

looters – robbers; people who steal objects of value

maize – Indian corn; the main food crop of the Maya

maritime – relating to the sea or shipping

Mesoamerica – Middle America; a term used to describe an area from central Mexico south through Guatemala, Belize, Honduras, and El Salvador

mural – an image painted directly onto a wall

obsidian – a hard volcanic stone that can be sharpened and used as a blade

plaque – a thin, flat badge used for decoration

plaza – an open area in the middle of a city

reconstruction – a modern attempt to imagine how something appeared in ancient times

reliefs – carvings with a raised surface

rituals – repeated practices that relate to specific, often religious, ceremonies

sacrifice – an offering to the gods, often involving the killing of a person or animal

sarcophagus – a stone coffin

scribe – an official whose job was to write out glyphs on stelae or manuscripts

stela – an upright stone slab carved with inscriptions; plural stelae

survey – a careful collection of data about an area or subject

theory – in science, the explanation that best explains all of the known facts

tomb – a place where a dead body is kept

Bibliography

Books

The Magnificent Maya (Lost Civilizations series). Alexandria, VA: Time-Life Books, 1993.

Wood, Marion. *Ancient Maya and Aztec Civilizations* (Cultural Atlas for Young People). New York: Chelsea House Publishers, 2007.

Articles

Demarest, Arthur A. "The Violent Saga of a Maya Kingdom." NATIONAL GEOGRAPHIC. (February 1993): 94–111.

Miller, Mary. "Maya Masterpiece Revealed at Bonampak." NATIONAL GEOGRAPHIC (February 1995): 50–69.

Saturno, William. "The Dawn of Maya Gods and Kings." NATIONAL GEOGRAPHIC (January 2006): 68–73.

Stuart, George S. "The Royal Crypts of Copán." NATIONAL GEOGRAPHIC (December 1997): 68–93.

Vesilind, Priit J. "Maya Water World." NATIONAL GEOGRAPHIC (October 2003): 82–101.

Further Reading

Coe, Michael D. *The Maya* (7th edition). New York: Thames and Hudson, 2005.

Perl, Lila. *Ancient Maya* (People of the Ancient World). New York: Franklin Watts, 2005.

Sharer, Robert, and Loa Traxler. *The Ancient Maya* (6th edition). Stanford, CA: Stanford University Press, 2005.

On the Web

About.com Maya archaeology links
http://archaeology.about.com/od/maya archaeology/Maya_Civilization.htm

Archaeology's Interactive Dig, Belize
http://www.archaeology.org/interactive/belize/index.html

Courtly Art of the Ancient Maya exhibit at the National Gallery of Art
http://www.nga.gov/exhibitions/mayainfo.shtm

Dig! The Maya Project, Dallas Museum of Art
http://dallasmuseumofart.org/dig/maya/index.htm

Historylink101 Maya Page
http://historylink101.com/1/mayan/ancient_mayan.htm

Index

About the Author

NATHANIEL HARRIS studied at University College, Oxford, before beginning a career in publishing. Since the publication of *Struggle for Supremacy* in 1969, he has been a full-time author specializing in historical subjects. Nathaniel Harris has written more than 60 books, including *Everyday Life in Ancient Egypt* and *Mummies*, advised on historical TV series, and contributed to numerous periodicals. He currently lives in the west of England.

Sources for Quotations

Page 37. Quoted in *The Magnificent Maya*. Alexandria, VA: Time-Life Books, 1993.

About the Consultant

ELIZABETH GRAHAM earned a Ph.D. in archaeology from Cambridge University before becoming a lecturer in Mesoamerican archaeology at University College, London. She has written widely about the Maya, and since 1988 has been the director of the field archaeology project at the Maya site of Lamanai in Belize.

> This terra cotta figure of a Maya warrior was found on a small island off the coast of the Yucatán, where the Maya built a graveyard for the elite during the Classic period. Many nobles were buried with small figures like this.

For information about special discounts for bulk purchases, contact National Geographic Special Sales: ngspecsales@ngs.org

One of the world's largest nonprofit scientific and educational organizations, the National Geographic Society was founded in 1888 "for the increase and diffusion of geographic knowledge." Fulfilling this mission, the Society educates and inspires millions every day through its magazines, books, television programs, videos, maps and atlases, research grants, the National Geographic Bee, teacher workshops, and innovative classroom materials. The Society is supported through membership dues, charitable gifts, and income from the sale of its educational products. This support is vital to National Geographic's mission to increase global understanding and promote conservation of our planet through exploration, research, and education.

For more information, please call 1-800-NGS-LINE (647-5463) or write to the following address:

National Geographic Society
1145 17th Street N.W.
Washington, D.C. 20036-4688
U.S.A.

Visit the Society's Web site:
www.nationalgeographic.com

Library of Congress Cataloging-in-Publication Data available upon request
Hardcover ISBN: 978-1-4263-0227-5
Library Edition ISBN: 978-1-4263-0228-2

Printed in Mexico

Series design by Jim Hiscott
The body text is set in Century Schoolbook
The display text is set in Helvetica Neue, Clarendon

National Geographic Society

John M. Fahey, Jr., *President and Chief Executive Officer;* Gilbert M. Grosvenor, *Chairman of the Board;* Nina D. Hoffman, *Executive Vice President; President of Book Publishing Group*

Staff for This Book

Nancy Laties Feresten, *Vice President, Editor-in-Chief of Children's Books*
Virginia Ann Koeth, *Project Editor*
Bea Jackson, *Director of Design and Illustration*
David M. Seager, *Art Director*
Lori Epstein, National Geographic Image Sales, *Illustrations Editors*
Jean Cantu, *Illustrations Specialist*
Priyanka Lamichhane, *Assistant Editor*

R. Gary Colbert, *Production Director*
Lewis R. Bassford, *Production Manager*
Maryclare Tracy, Nicole Elliott, *Manufacturing Managers*
Maps, *Mapping Specialists, Ltd.*

For the Brown Reference Group, plc

Tim Cooke, *Editor*
Alan Gooch, *Book Designer*
Laila Torsun, *Picture Researcher*
Encompass Graphics, *Cartographers*
Kay Ollerenshaw, *Indexer*

Photo Credits

Front cover: A vessel in the shape of a human head for burning incense during religious rituals
Page 1 and back cover: A terra-cotta container in the shape of a god with a cornflower
Pages 2–3: Dawn rises over a settlement of thatched homes built by descendants of the Maya in Chiapas state, Mexico.